# Welcome Savings Starter

**If you close your eyes** and think about money, what do you see? Do you see stacks of dollar bills? A piggy bank full of nickels, dimes, and quarters that jingle when you shake it? Or do you see yourself in a store buying something special?

Money is all of these things and more. That's what you will find when you read *Savings Starter*. This book is full of puzzles, games, and fun facts about money. Do you like history? Let's go back in time to learn why people invented money. Do you ever wonder what all the pictures on money mean? You may be surprised at what you see when you take a tour of a dollar bill.

So let's turn the page and learn more about earning, saving, and spending MONEY.

## STANDARD & POOR'S

McGraw Hill Glencoe

New York, New York    Columbus, Ohio    Chicago, Illinois    Peoria, Illinois    Woodland Hills, California

STANDARD
&POOR'S

Mc Graw Hill  **Glencoe**





Send all inquiries to:
Glencoe/McGraw-Hill
21600 Oxnard Street, Suite 500
Woodland Hills, California 91367-4906

ISBN 0-07-868224-X

1 2 3 4 5 6 7 8 9  079  09 08 07 06 05 04

# Contents

**W**hy did people invent money? Money was invented because people wanted a way to trade things they had for things they wanted. Say you have an apple orchard and you pick apples every day to eat. One day you get tired of eating apples. You decide you want some oranges instead. Luckily for you an orange-grower lives down the street. You knock on his door with a basket of apples and minutes later you leave with your oranges. Success! The trade you just made is an example of **bartering,** or giving away one thing to get another.

You may have bartered yourself. Have you ever switched lunches with a friend at school or traded baseball cards? These are both examples of bartering.

But what happens if you try to barter with someone who doesn't want what you have? Let's pretend again that you have an apple orchard. But instead of trading your apples for oranges, you want a new kite. You go to the kite maker and offer to trade apples for a kite, but the kite maker doesn't like apples. You and the kite maker need to agree on something else to trade. That's why money was invented. Money is an item that people agree to use for trade.

Throughout history, money has taken on many different forms. Seashells, salt, tea, cattle, even whale teeth and elephant hair have been used as money in different parts of the world.

**2500 B.C.**
Egyptians used metal rings as money.

**400 B.C.**
Greeks started using coins they called drachmas. Today they use coins called euros.

**1275**
Italian explorer Marco Polo found paper money being used in China.

## The First Coins

Thousands of years ago, people began using chunks of gold, silver, and copper as money. The Egyptians used metal rings for money. In ancient Lydia, an area that is now the country of Turkey, people started making and using the first metal coins. The Greeks and Romans passed coins on to later cultures in other parts of the world. The use of coins spread quickly as people traveled around the world buying and selling things.

## The First Paper Money

Coins were easier for people to carry around than, say, a bag of elephant hair or a handful of seashells. But coins were also easy to lose. So instead of carrying coins, people started leaving them in a safe place. Today we call this place a bank. In ancient times, the "banker" would give the owner of the coins a piece of paper, or "note," with the value of the coins written on it. This note was much lighter to carry and it was worth as much as the coins. When the coin-owner bought or sold something, the bank note was passed from person to person. The note could be exchanged for coins by bringing it back to the bank. These "bank notes" were the start of paper money.

In the United States, the coins we usually use today are pennies (1¢), nickels (5¢), dimes (10¢), and quarters (25¢). The "¢" symbol means cents. Our paper money is called dollars. Most of our paper money is in $1, $5, $10, $20, $50, and $100 notes (the "$" symbol means dollars).

**1690**
The first paper money was used in the American colonies.

**1700-1800**
Coins were being used as money throughout Europe.

**1862**
The U.S. Treasury began printing United States Notes, or "greenbacks." Today we still get our dollars from the U.S. Treasury.

# WHAT'S *a budget?*

**S**pending money can be fun. If you receive money from an allowance, for chores you do around the house, or from a paper route, you may have some **spending money**. If you don't stop to think before you buy, you may end up spending money on things you don't really need.

Instead, you can plan how to spend your money. This plan is called a **budget**. Your budget can help you save up your spending money to buy things that may cost more than you have right now. For example, suppose your allowance is $5 per week and you want to buy a video game that costs $40. If you save your allowance for three weeks, you would have $15 saved. If you save for six weeks, you would have $30 saved. And after eight weeks you would have $40 — enough to buy your video game.

But what if you want to save money for something expensive, and you also want to spend some of your money right now? You can see how a budget works on the next page.

# How a Budget Works

A budget is a list of the money you think you will receive or earn and how you plan to spend it. You can make a budget for one week, one month, or a whole year! Read the steps and sample answers below, then make your own budget on page 9.

**Step 1:** Under "Income" write down the amount of money you receive each week and where it comes from — your allowance, as a gift, or from another place.

SAMPLE

Income:

From: ___allowance___    Amount: ___$5.00___

From: ___raking leaves___    Amount: ___$5.00___  +

Add up the Income amounts: ___$10.00___ = Total Income

**Step 2:** Under "Expenses" write down what you plan to spend your money on each week and how much each thing will cost.

SAMPLE

Expenses:

Item: ___trading cards___    Amount: ___$2.00___

Item: ___comic book___    Amount: ___$1.80___  +

Add up the Expense amounts: ___$3.80___ = Total Expenses

**Step 3:** How much will you save for things you want to buy later on? To find out, subtract your Total Expenses from your Total Income.

Total Income: ___$10.00___ – Total Expenses: ___$3.80___ = Savings: ___$6.20___

# Save for What You Want

**1** Set goals for your savings. Examples of goals might be buying small things like a birthday gift for your sister, or a big thing like a new bicycle. Write down some of your goals:

_a new soccer ball, a gift for Katie's birthday_

_________________________________________________________________

_________________________________________________________________

**2** Now find out how much each goal will cost. The next time you see an item you want to buy, find out what the price is and write it down on the lines below. For instance, if your goal is to buy a soccer ball and the amount you need to save is $28, you can buy it after seven weeks if you save $4 a week:

$$7 \times \$4.00 = \$28.00$$

Goal:_________________ Amount to save:_________________

Goal:_________________ Amount to save:_________________

Goal:_________________ Amount to save:_________________

Goal:_________________ Amount to save:_________________

Goal:_________________ Amount to save:_________________

**3** How long will you need to save to reach your goals? To find out, fill in the budget on page 9 to see how much you plan to save each week.

The more you save, the faster you'll reach your goal!

# Make Your Own Budget!

Use the space below to make your own budget.
Ask an adult to check your work.

### Step 1: Income

Write down the amount of money you receive each week and where it comes from — your allowance, as a gift, or from another place.

From:_______________ Amount:_______________

From:_______________ Amount:_______________

From:_______________ Amount:_______________

From:_______________ Amount:_______________

From:_______________ Amount:_______________

From:_______________ Amount:_______________

Add up the Income amounts: _____________ = Total Income

### Step 2: Expenses

Write down what you plan to spend your money on each week and how much each thing will cost.

Item:_______________ Amount:_______________

Item:_______________ Amount:_______________

Item:_______________ Amount:_______________

Item:_______________ Amount:_______________

Item:_______________ Amount:_______________

Add up the Expense amounts: _____________ = Total Expenses

### Step 3: Savings

How much will you save for things you want to buy later on? To find out, subtract your Total Expenses from your Total Income.

Total Income: _______ – Total Expenses: _______ = Savings:_______

# Key Words to Find

| | | | |
|---|---|---|---|
| ~~ATM~~ | Coins | Invest | Profit |
| Bank | Dime | Loan | Quarter |
| Budget | Dollar | Money | Savings |
| Cash | Euro | Nickel | Ten |
| Cents | Five | Penny | Yen |
| Check | Interest | Pound | |

```
D R A L L O D A I P I W
N P R O F I T C N N N Y
S A V I N G S E V N T Y
E Y S D D C V N E C E N
U V E I N O A T S H R E
R D M M U I N S T E P T
O R O E O N L I H C S P
T E N U P S T V C K T E
I L E K C I N P N E E G
O A Y N N L O A N Y V D
N E Y E A R B N T E I U
D T R E T R A U Q M F B
```

Circle all the words you find scrambled in this box. Remember, words might be printed forward, backward, or on an angle.

Answers are on page 24.

# Green backs

The first paper bills used in America were called "greenbacks" because they were printed in green ink.

# Where are YOUR spondulicks?

Spondulicks is just one nickname for money in the United States. Other terms for money that you can try out on your friends include gelt, long green, and simoleons.

# Our money is Shrinking!

A dollar bill is 6.14 inches wide and 2.61 inches tall. That's smaller than it was before 1929, when the dollar was 7.42 inches wide and 3.125 inches tall.

# A Year in the Life...

A $1 bill lasts about one year before it wears out. A $10 or $20 bill lasts longer, and buys more!

# Behind the MONEY MACHINE

Those **bank machines** seem like *magic,* don't they? Your parents put a card in the slot, and out **POPS** money.

You know by now that your parents are simply taking out of the bank what they already put in there. While it's in the bank, it's GROWING as well — and you can grow your money there too. Here's how...

## How Your Money Grows

Now that you know how to save, you can begin by putting some of this money in a piggy bank or jar in your room. The money in your "piggy" doesn't grow, but it's there when you need it.

When you have a few dollars saved, ask your parents to help you open your own **savings account** at a bank or credit union. These are places that keep your money safe — and also help it grow. When you open a savings account, you'll be given a **passbook** that lists all of the money you put in and take out.

While your money is in a savings account, **interest** is added. Interest is money that the bank or credit union pays you for keeping money there.

For example, let's say a bank promises to add "3% interest" every month to any money in your account. That means each month you'll get an extra 3 cents for each dollar you have in your account. Your money, plus any interest, is there when you need it.

You can buy what you need with U.S. dollars anywhere in America. But if you buy something in another country, you have to use that country's **currency,** which is another word for money. Money from other countries comes in many sizes and colors. It may seem funny to you, but it's money just the same.

$ If you go to **Switzerland** to buy some cheese, you have to pay for it in *francs*, not dollars.

$ If you go to a baseball game in **Japan**, you must buy your ticket with *yen*.

$ If you go to **England** to ride on a big red bus, you have to pay the driver in *pounds*.

$ If you buy lunch in **Italy** or some other countries in Europe, you have to pay with *euros*.

$ If you go to **Russia** to ride the train, you must buy your ticket with *rubles*.

$ If you have some extra *pesos*, you might go to a soccer game in **Argentina**.

Answers to Funny Money quiz on page 24.

**Now test your memory. Draw a line to connect each country to its currency.**

| | |
|---|---|
| Russia | dollars |
| Argentina | rubles |
| Switzerland | pounds |
| Japan | euros |
| Italy | pesos |
| England | francs |
| United States | yen |

# World Wide Web games

- H.I.P. Pocket Change (http://www.usmint.gov/kids) — check out the fun you can have with coins and try the animated games or the time machine. (ages 6 and up)
- The Lemonade Stand Game (http://www.coolmath4kids.com/lemonade) — get some practice at "running" your own business. (ages 8 and up)
- Escape From Knab (http://www.escapefromknab.com) — to escape from the strange and slimy planet Knab, you need to raise $10,000 for a ticket back to earth.
- The Cash register Game (http://www.funbrain.com/cashreg) — do the math and win. Are you a superbrain? If you are, watch your piggy bank grow as you figure out the correct change.

# GAMES ON MONEY

If you're looking for a new game to play, and a way to learn more about the world of money, take a look at these ideas. You can ask for these as gifts or save up and buy them for yourself.

- The Game of Life (about $15) — learn about college loans, mortgages, car insurance, dividends, and taxes. (ages 9 and up)
- Payday ($15) — if you ever wonder why your parents groan about "paying the bills," then this game is for you. (ages 8 and up)
- Monopoly ($10) — here you can buy land, build hotels, and go to jail, all in one game. (ages 8 and up)
- Monopoly Jr. ($10) — a shorter version of Monopoly (above), where you buy amusement park rides instead of houses and hotels. (ages 5 to 8)

# "Mega-money"

The first paper money was used in China more than 600 years ago. It was made of tree bark and was as big as a sheet of notebook paper!

# Bank
## Accountable

The word "bank" comes from the Italian word *banca* which means bench. This is where money lenders sat in the markets in Rome.

# The Face Facts

George Washington's picture is on the $1 bill. What other famous people have their pictures on our money?

$5 — Abraham Lincoln, the 16th president of the United States

$10 — Alexander Hamilton, a leader of the American Revolution

$20 — Andrew Jackson, the 7th president of the United States

# What Do You Call...

$10,000,000,000,
000,000,000,000,
000,000,000,000,
000,000,000,000,
000,000,000,000,
000,000,000,000,
000,000,000,000,
000,000,000,000,
000,000?

## Googol-dollars
### of course!

The term "googol" — which describes the number 1 followed by 100 zeroes — was created by the 9-year old nephew of Edward Kasner, the mathematician who popularized the phrase.

# What's on Your Dollar?

You may have a one-dollar bill, or maybe two, in your pocket right now. You probably know that it's green and has some pictures on it. But have you ever looked at a dollar *very carefully* to see what's printed on it? Come take a tour of a one-dollar bill. You might be surprised at what you see.

The front of every dollar has a long number in green ink that appears in two places. This is called a **serial number**. Every dollar ever printed has a different number.

We use **dollars** to buy things and to pay back **money** that we borrow. To remind us of this, a notice on the front of every dollar says: "This note is legal tender for all debts, public and private."

**note** = paper money
**tender** = payment
**debt** = money owed

The year this bill was **printed**

A picture of **George Washington**, the first president of the United States, is on the front of every one-dollar bill. Which famous Americans are pictured on the $5, $10, and $20 bills? (Check your answer on page 15.)



Adapted from *The Go-Around Dollar*, Simon & Schuster Books, 1992. Used with permission.

# Quiz:

Look closely at a dollar bill. Can you count the number of times the number "1" and word "one" appear on the front and back?
*Answer to Quiz on page 24.*

On the back of every dollar is the **Great Seal of the United States,** an important national symbol. The two sides of the seal are in circles. One circle has an **eagle** in it. The other circle has a **pyramid**.
The Great Seal contains two Latin mottos:
**Annuit Coeptis** — "He has favored our undertaking."
**Novus Ordo Seclorum** — "A new order of centuries."

The unfinished pyramid represents **growth** in the **future**, while the eye atop the pyramid symbolizes the helpful gaze of God.

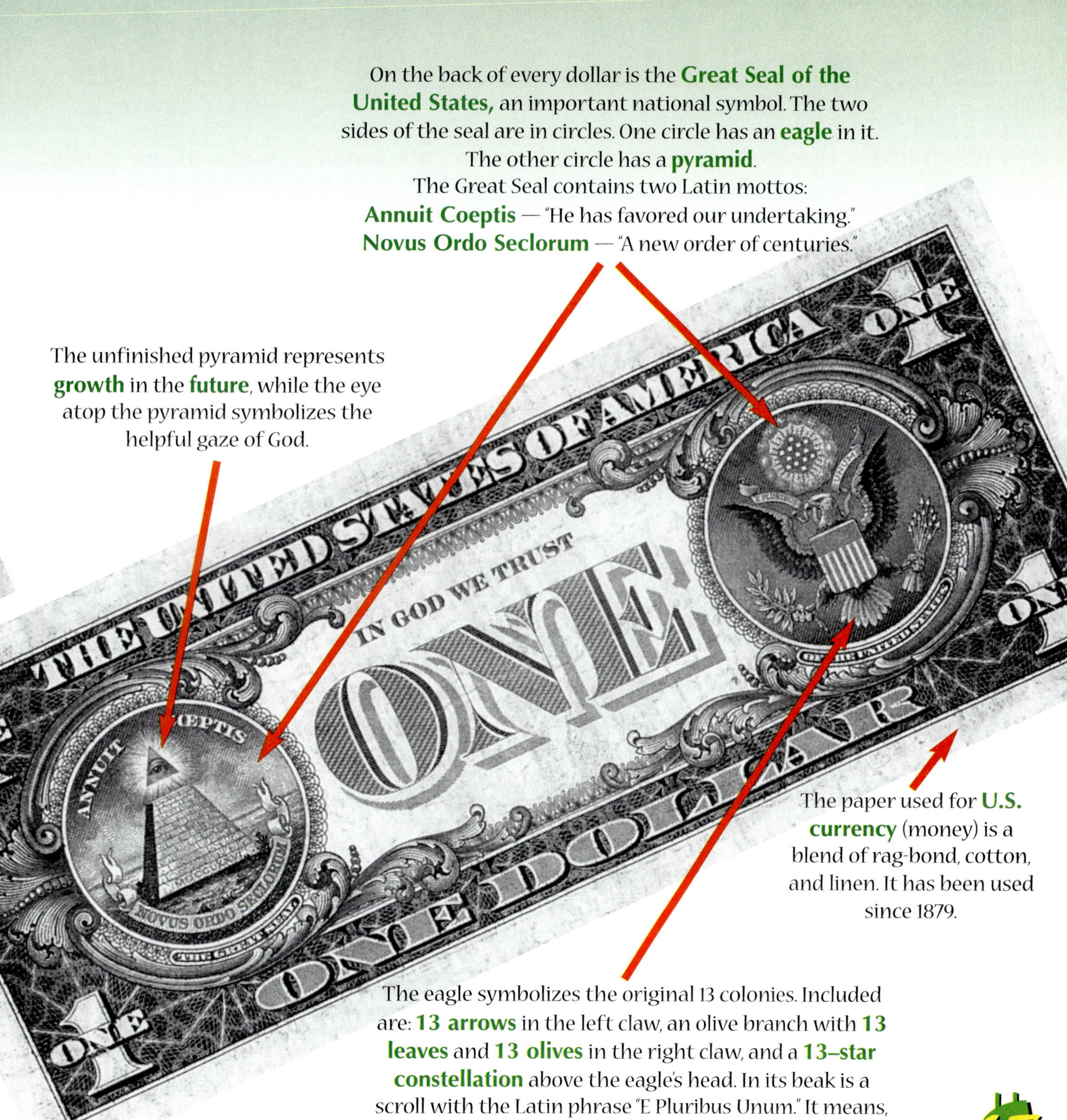

The paper used for **U.S. currency** (money) is a blend of rag-bond, cotton, and linen. It has been used since 1879.

The eagle symbolizes the original 13 colonies. Included are: **13 arrows** in the left claw, an olive branch with **13 leaves** and **13 olives** in the right claw, and a **13–star constellation** above the eagle's head. In its beak is a scroll with the Latin phrase "E Pluribus Unum." It means, "From many, one."

# Dollars & ¢ents

Pennies, nickels, dimes, quarters, and half dollars are smaller pieces of one dollar.

penny.......................... 1 cent
nickel........................ 5 cents
dime........................ 10 cents
quarter................. 25 cents
half dollar............ 50 cents

## Do you know how many of each it would take to make one dollar?

_________ pennies = 1 dollar

_________ nickels = 1 dollar

_________ dimes = 1 dollar

_________ quarters = 1 dollar

_________ half dollars = 1 dollar

## Can you figure out the totals of the coins provided?

Two quarters and one dime =

_________________________

One half dollar and four dimes =

_________________________

Six dimes, one penny, and five nickels =

_________________________

(The answers are on page 21.)

# THE MATCH GAME

**BARTER**

**PASSBOOK**

**INCOME**

**BUDGET**

**SAVINGS ACCOUNT**

**CURRENCY**

**INTEREST**

A written plan for spending and saving money

Money that a bank or credit union pays you to keep your money there

When you trade one item for another

A safe place to keep your money where it will be able to grow

Another word for money

A book that lists all of the money you put in and take out of your savings account

The amount of money you receive as an allowance, or earn by working

(Answers to The Match Game are on page 24.)

# Money Scrabble

Fill in the squares with answers to the clues.

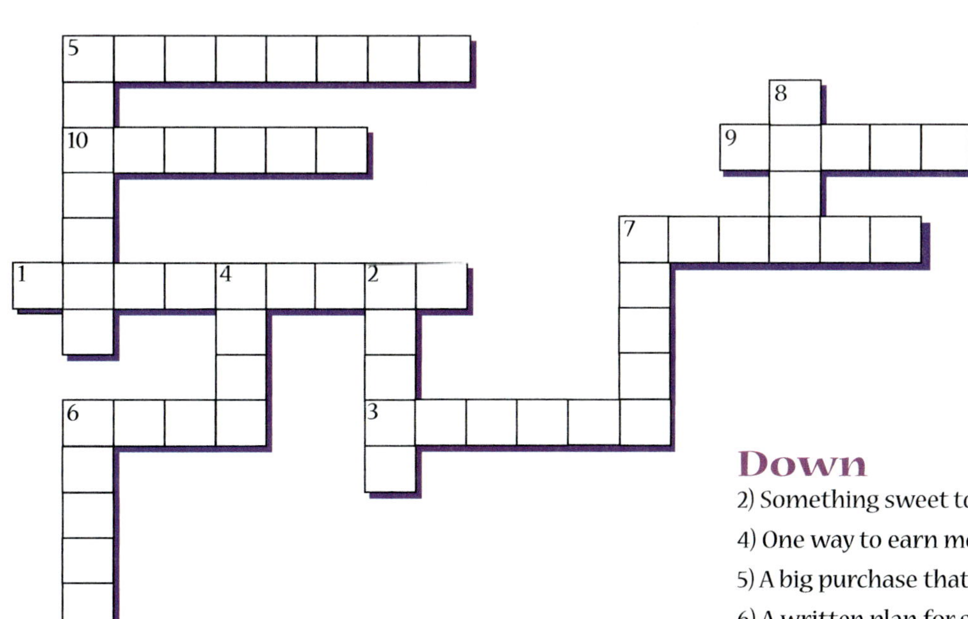

(Answers to Money Scrabble are on page 24.)

## Across

1) Money you may receive from your parents every day, week, or month.

3) One hundred pennies is the same as one __________.

5) Your special day to receive cards and gifts.

6) Feed your piggy __________ pennies.

7) You might save to buy a gift for your father or mother, or a brother or a __________.

9) Five dimes is the same as __________ cents.

10) To pay for something that costs more or less than one dollar bill, you have to make __________.

## Down

2) Something sweet to eat.

4) One way to earn money is to __________.

5) A big purchase that will take you for a ride.

6) A written plan for spending and saving money.

7) The opposite of a spender is a __________.

8) One way to receive money is as a __________.

# A-MAZE-ING! SAVING

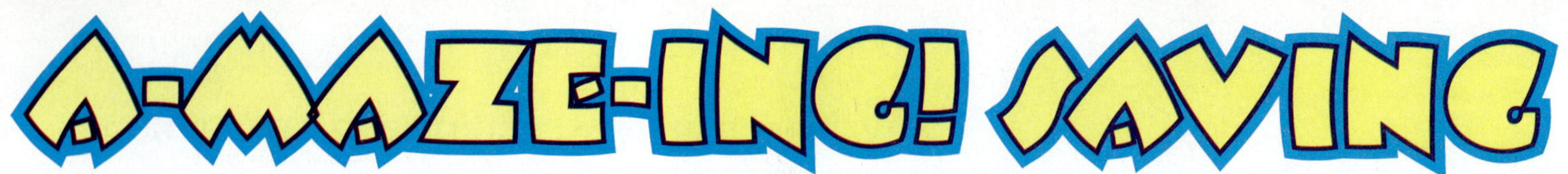

Samantha isn't very good at saving her money. She spends too much of her hard-earned cash on things like bubble gum and candy, and doesn't save enough for the things she really wants.

## Help Samantha put her money in her piggy bank without stopping to spend on the things she doesn't really need.

Draw a line through the maze from Samantha to the piggy bank without passing through any of the goodies.

Caution: You may want to use a pencil on this maze because saving money isn't as easy as it seems.

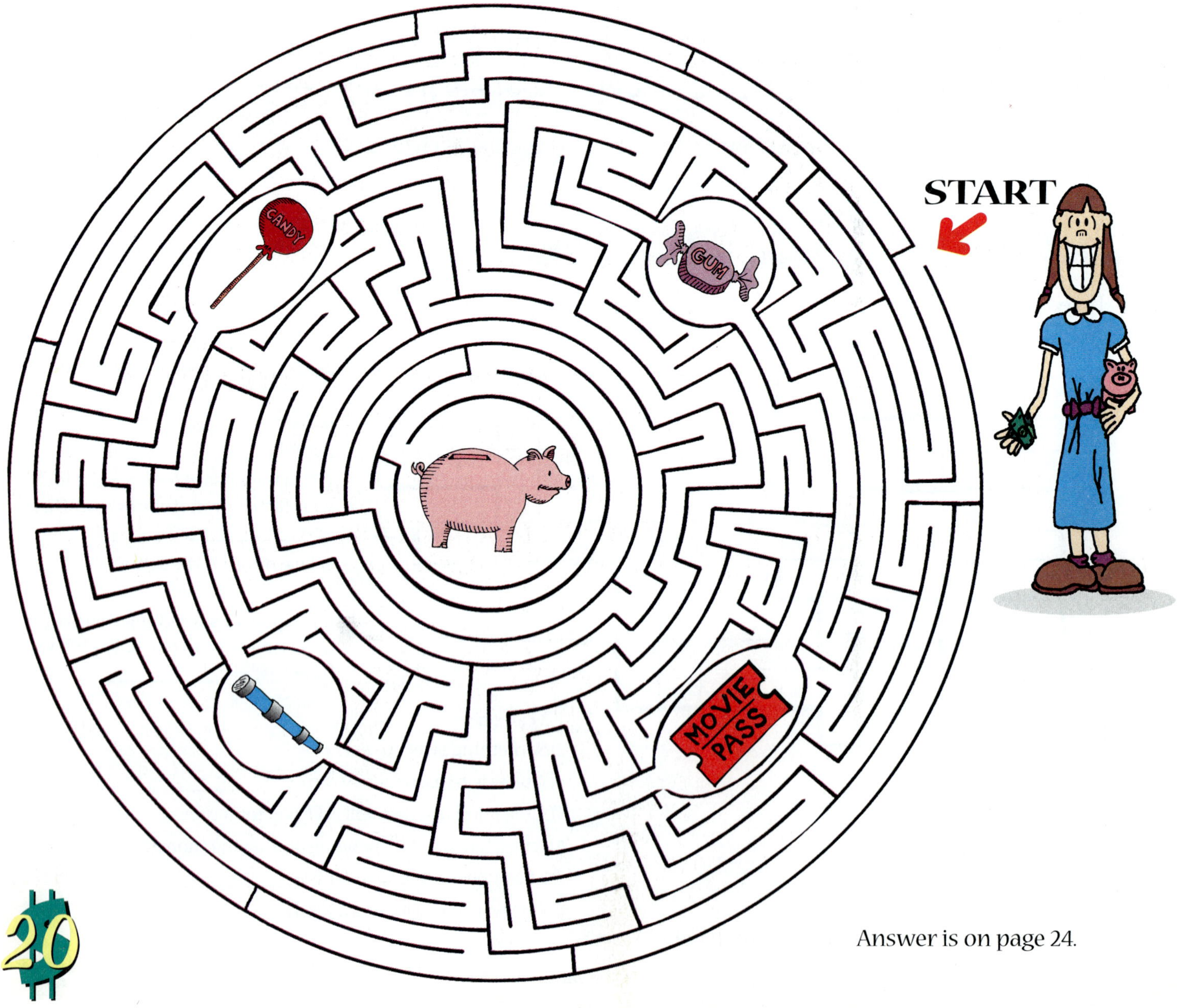


Answer is on page 24.

**Saving for the things you want to buy and do is easy. It just takes a little planning and time. This chart shows how long you will need to save for those special items on your wish list.**

# The Price Is Right

## If you save $5.00 per week...

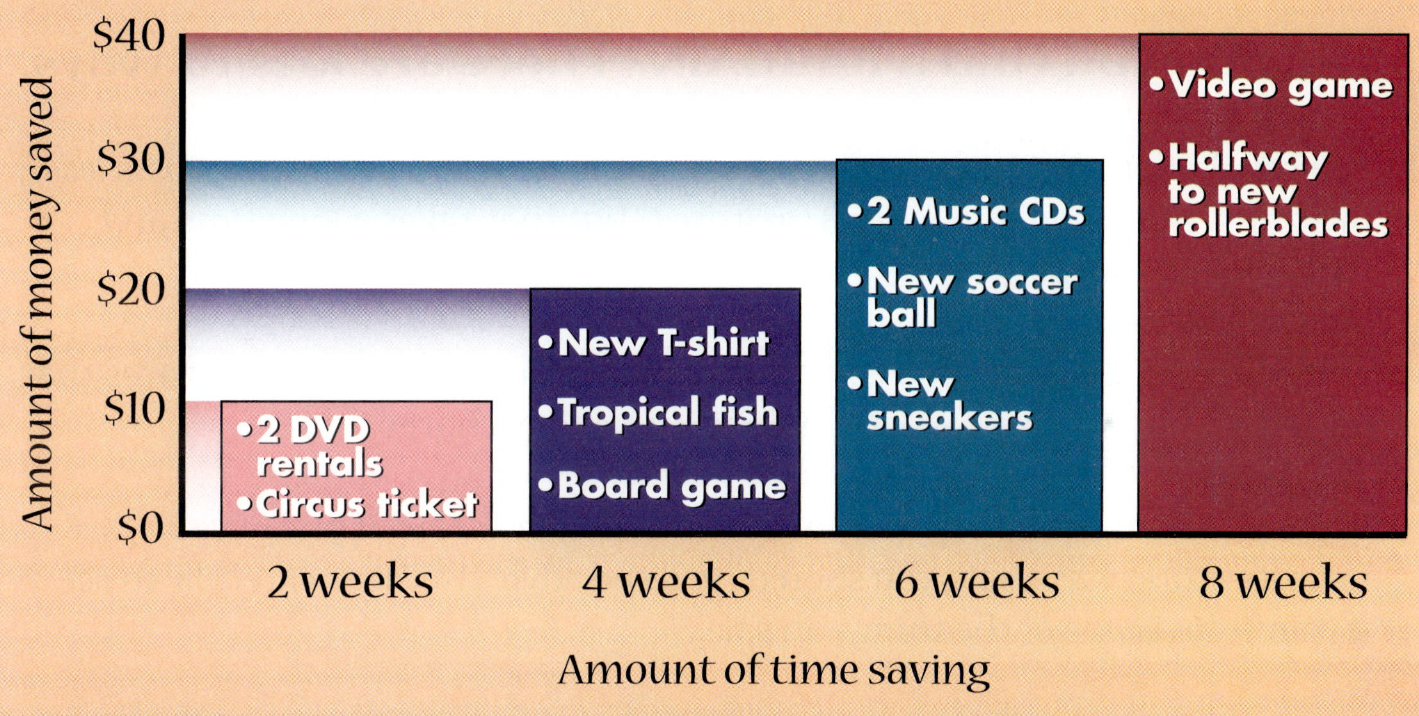


Answers to "Dollars & Cents" (on page 18):

100 pennies = 1 dollar

20 nickels = 1 dollar

10 dimes = 1 dollar

4 quarters = 1 dollar

2 half dollars = 1 dollar

Two quarters and one dime =
60 cents = 60¢

One half dollar and four dimes =
90 cents = 90¢

Six dimes, one penny and five nickels =
86 cents = 86¢

## How do you find a BARGAIN? There are lots of ways.

✔ You can go to more than one store to see if the item you are buying costs less in Store A than it does in Store B or Store C, but that takes a long time and makes your feet tired.

✔ Before you go shopping, you could call (or ask an adult to call) some stores that have the item you want. Ask them how much they charge for it.

✔ You can look in the newspaper for stores that have "sales." If one of your favorite stores has a sale, you should read the advertisement carefully to see if your item is one of the things on sale.

You can keep track of the prices of different things at different stores on a chart like this:

## The SmartKid Shopping Sheet

| What I want to buy | Price at Store A | Price at Store B | Price at Store C |
| --- | --- | --- | --- |
| New sneakers | $25 | $28.50 | $32 |
| | | | |
| | | | |
| | | | |

# 7 *tips for becoming a ...* SUPERSAVER



You may already be a good saver. But if you follow some of these tips, you could become a super saver!

**1.** Save first, spend later. If you save after you spend, you may not save at all. When you save, you eventually have the power to buy what you want.

**2.** Save at least 25 cents out of every dollar you receive. That means if you get a dollar in allowance, save 25 cents or more. If you get five dollars, save at least $1.25.

**3.** You can only spend money once! So make sure you really want or need what you buy.

**4.** Don't carry all of your money when you go shopping. Take just what you think you will need. If you don't have it with you, you can't spend it.

**5.** Count your money. It's fun to watch your savings grow and it will keep you interested in saving.

**6.** When you have some money saved in your piggy bank, ask an adult to help you open a savings account or deposit your money in the bank.

**7.** Ask your parents to pay your allowance in "small money" — dollar bills and quarters. That way it's easier to divide the money you save between a piggy bank and your savings account.

# ANSWERS

## PAGE 10 KEY WORDS TO FIND

## PAGE 17 WHAT'S ON YOUR DOLLAR QUIZ

There are a total of sixteen "1s/ones" on a dollar bill.

## PAGE 13 FUNNY MONEY QUIZ

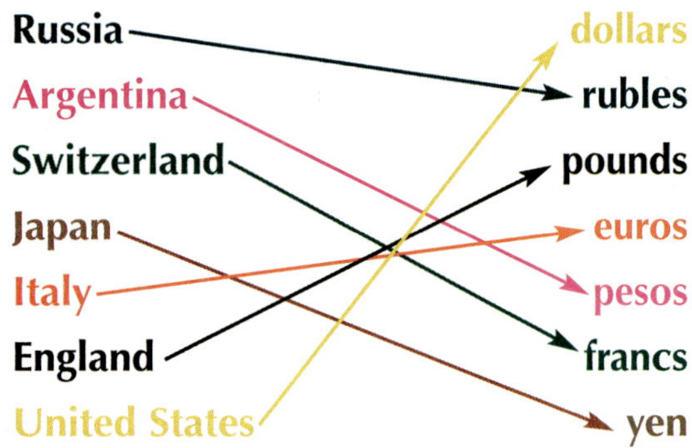


## PAGE 19 THE MATCH GAME

## PAGE 20 A-MAZE-ING! SAVING

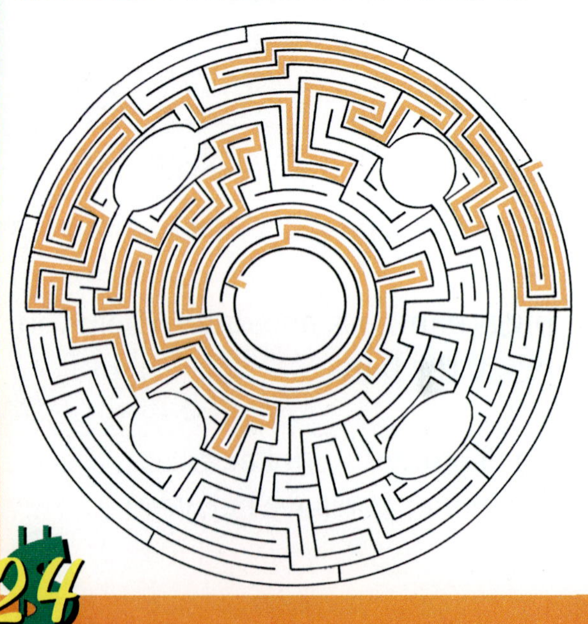

## PAGE 19 MONEY SCRABBLE

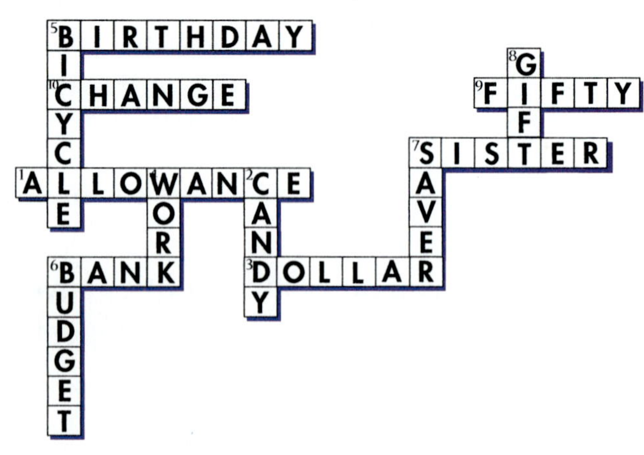